Only
YOU
can
make
YOU
happy

John C. Tormey

LIGUORI
PUBLICATIONS

One Liguori Drive
Liguori, Missouri 63057-9999
(314) 464-2500

Imprimi Potest:
Daniel L. Lowery, C.SS.R.
Provincial, St. Louis Province
Redemptorist Fathers

Imprimatur:
+ Charles R. Koester, S.T.D.
Vicar General, Archdiocese of St. Louis

Published by Liguori Publications
Printed in U.S.A. 1975

Contents

Introduction 5

1. Potential 7

2. Problems 12

3. People 17

4. Identity 24

5. Ideas 28

6. Involvement 33

7. Experience 38

8. Energy 44

9. Excellence 50

10. The Ultimate Answer 57

Dedicated to
Bud and Marilyn McAuliffe —
happy people who enjoy life.

Introduction

"Pie in the sky" is an expression often used to indicate heavenly bliss. It seems to suggest that real happiness is not to be found on this earth but only in the afterlife.

This is true in our quest for total happiness, but in the meantime we can experience many relatively happy days. It all depends on whether we really "desire" to be happy.

With St. Paul:

We are often troubled, but not crushed
Sometimes in doubt, but never in despair
With many enemies, but never without a friend
Badly hurt at times, but not destroyed.

In the words of Abraham Lincoln: "People are as happy as they make up their minds to be."

This booklet of prayerful thoughts offers the same challenge. It is a call to excellence, and in the response we attain the happiness that comes from satisfaction.

The song "Georgy Girl" was a smash hit some years ago. It described a young girl — lonely, unhappy, and confused.

She had a great deal of happiness hidden deep in her personality. Challenged to bring out her real self, she dreams of the someone she could be.

She recognizes that life is a reality and that she can't always run away. So, she tells herself not to be scared of changing and rearranging herself. And she thinks it's time she jumps down from the shelf.

The 90 reflections in this book do not guarantee happiness, but they do issue the call to change and rearrange, to jump down from the shelf. We can be more than a spectator of someone else's happiness. We can enjoy this life, too.

The first three chapters accentuate the development of our personal potential. The middle three concentrate on our personal identity. The last three offer the challenge to excellence.

Each reflection is an unlit match. One of them may strike and ignite a warm flame of enthusiasm within you. I hope it happens.

Chapter 1

POTENTIAL

Everyone has inside himself . . .
A piece of good news!
The good news is that you really don't know
   how great you can be
   how much you can love
   what you can accomplish
   what your potential is.
How can you top good news like that? — Anne Frank

People on an average use only 10 percent of their creative potential. They do not develop more than the minimum and yet they have resources to attain the maximum. They groan for fulfillment but fail to meet the challenge of their own power because they lack the basic *desire* to be better than they are.

The secret of becoming a great person is as easy as desiring it. For "desire" means "to wish earnestly, to crave, to yearn, to long for."

There is the story told of a master and his student who were studying a great truth. The student just could not comprehend. In desperation, the master grabbed the student and put his head under water. At the very last second the master pulled him from death. He asked the student what he was thinking when he was under water. "I desired air," he answered. The master responded, "So then you must desire truth and you will receive it." We too must desire to become better than we are; then we will be able to develop our potential.

Wonderment, curiosity, and adventure are the vital signs of an interesting life. When we are interested in the many experiences of life, each day is a challenge. We awake with the thrilling feeling of learning something new, and fulfilling something we could not accomplish yesterday.

Interest must come from our own impetus, however. We create it with pure desire and participation. It grows from the feeling that we have a contribution to make so we will not let this day pass without accomplishing something.

We tap our potential every time we humbly say: "I know that I do not know." We no longer pretend to be already fulfilled, so we yearn for the opportunity to listen and learn.

Pettiness endangers potential because it causes boredom. It drains our life of wonderment, enthusiasm, risk, and expansion. When we expand and broaden our personality, we allow a whole new experience of adventure to come pouring in.

Many people are ill content because they are just not excited about anything. They have stopped learning. They have a paucity of ideas and interests, and therefore they have little motivation. They live their day with petty conversation and superficial activity.

One cure for boredom is a constant pursuit of learning. Knowledge refreshes the mind, recreates the spirit, and motivates the body. It creates the enthusiasm and desire to live an exciting and full day in spite of routine.

Life is not dull. We make it dull by limiting our potential and stifling our interests with pettiness.

It is scientifically proven that there are certain viruses that live in us and cause disease when the defenses of our body wear down. The same is true of our spirit. When our spirit is tired and apathetic we are susceptible to a *dis − ease*. The only remedy is the desire to develop our potential. The more fulfilled we are, the happier we are.

An automobile can ordinarily be driven for many miles, but abuse and constant racing will burn out the engine. The same is true for our mind and body. We must pace our life to meet its many demands with the norm of relative moderation. Otherwise we will burn out very quickly. Tension and anxiety are the telltale signs.

The Book of Sirach reminds us: "Be moderate in all your activities and illness will not overtake you." Anxiety and lack of peace is an illness. A person at peace has come to grips with his limitations of time, energy, and talent. He realizes that he is only human and must measure out his life gradually.

We all have big plans but we are also conditioned by limitations. When we awake each morning we should not over plan our daily schedule. We should keep some distance between our plans so that we will have time and energy to accomplish them.

Chapter 2

PROBLEMS

Would that we all lived in Camelot! But real life is not like that. Each day someone has to meet a problem head on — whether it be sickness, death, or unemployment. We all have our turns, but we cannot stop living. Many are the problems that can be solved by just living them out.

We must come to realize that there are some mysteries we cannot answer, some problems we cannot solve, some situations that will never be agreeable, but we can be happy in spite of them. The secret word is acceptance. If we can do something about the problem, fine. If we cannot, then we accept it and learn to live with it. Reinhold Niebuhr has written a beautiful prayer that we should make our own:

God grant me
SERENITY to accept the things I cannot change
COURAGE to change the things I can and
WISDOM to know the difference.

We make mountains out of molehills. With a false sense of proportion we make minor incidents into major catastrophes. If we must worry, we should save it for the big problems.

Often the greater portion of our anxiety comes from the anticipation of something that never happens, or from a minor disappointment that we magnify out of proportion. A truly wise adage for our daily living is: "Don't sweat the small stuff."

If we look back over our life, we'll find it hard to realize that we have allowed so many small disappointments to worry us in such a big way. With a sense of proportion, we'll never let it happen again.

There is nothing so overwhelming that we cannot handle, but for extra help we could make this prayer a daily experience:

O Lord, help me to remember that nothing is going to happen to me today that you and I together cannot handle.

Physical ailments, rejection, depression, anxiety — these are inevitable realities of the human condition. We can let them tear us apart or we can accept them for what they are. They *can* transform, mature, and educate us.

Acceptance should absorb pain like a sponge. It comes from the overwhelming desire to enjoy life in spite of suffering. It neither lashes out in blame nor turns inwardly toward self-pity. It realizes that suffering is an experience of the human condition, and if we are to "feel human" we must "feel suffering."

Jesus said: "My peace I give to you. My peace I leave with you"; then he submitted himself to suffering. He didn't suppress, explain, or justify it. Suffering offers a detachment and a transcendence. It makes all our material possessions seem so unimportant and frees us to go beyond them and find the real value of living.

Nervousness, restlessness, anxiety, yawning, running eyes, sweating, "gooseflesh," muscle twitching, hot and cold flashes, severe aches of back and legs, vomiting, diarrhea, and a feeling of desperation: All these complications characterize a withdrawal from opiates. What great joy — a momentary escape from reality only to face new problems!

Withdrawal from life is the result of our failure to cope with ideas — ideas of ourselves, unreal ideas of others, or ideas that bear responsibilities. Hallucinations seem more inviting because they are not real.

We become a mixture of artificial ideas, moods, and feelings that tear us apart. Once we lose control of our realness, our life will be a continual "cop out." We'll find a pill or bottle for everything because fear has become our master.

When we pause and enjoy silence, we discover answers and clarifications that activity does not have time to reveal. We put ourself together again.

Take three minute vacations. To vacate means to empty out. Get rid of your anxieties and tensions. Relax and reenergize. Take time out to stretch. It does wonders for the nervous system.

Recreation "creates again." It refreshes the mind, renews the spirit, and motivates the body. Activity can go wild unless we control it by integrating it with rest and relaxation.

Everyone needs a quiet center within himself — like the depth of the ocean. When a hurricane comes the fish go to the bottom of the ocean and wait it out. If we develop a desire for silence in our life we can wait out many problems — not by escaping but by pausing and absorbing.

Chapter 3

PEOPLE

We will meet many people who are miserable and who attempt to manipulate our happiness. Manipulation means that a person "puts his hand into our life and turns us around to his way of thinking." The power he has to ruin our personal happiness is in the power we give him.

If we desire to be happy and at peace today, then we should not turn over the power of manipulation to anyone. Misery enjoys company, and every miserable, bitter, and sarcastic person we meet can manipulate our peaceful life style if we are not careful.

Our best reaction is to remain happy so that they feel uncomfortable being miserable. We will not always find ourselves in a totally comfortable relationship, but the mature person manages to work things out without losing his cool.

No one can satisfy everyone all the time, and we'll wear ourselves down with nervous tension if we try. We should build on the premise that everyone is different and thus develop a realistic expectation of how people will react. We cannot expect to live by our convictions and fully satisfy everyone.

REAL PEOPLE

Respect

Every person as unique and become

Aware of how he feels by

Listening

The real person is free and open-minded, but he realizes that he cannot please or agree with everyone. His inner peace comes from the satisfaction that he is open and trying to do the best he can.

I'm sure Jesus often greeted others with the word "Shalom," which not only means peace but also wholeness and fullness. Shalom hopes the very best for a person. It is difficult for us to enjoy everyone, but we can hope that each receives the best of what life offers.

Cardinal Suenens describes the full meaning of shalom when he says:

The greatest good we can do for others is not to give them of our wealth but to show them their own.

Shalom brings us beyond the horizon of our own ideas and idiosyncrasies. We begin to tolerate other people. We do not attempt to form them into our shadow. We encourage them to develop their own talents. They have a fullness and potential all of their own. We might not agree with their ideas or life style but at least we are happy that they are becoming themselves.

Everyone needs a few close friends with whom to share intimate thoughts and to entrust secrets.

Unfortunately we cannot develop this closeness with everyone, so we must choose. Of all our friends, who will help us to become more appreciative of life and more enthusiastic about celebrating its wonders?

A friend should be chosen slowly and very carefully. As George Washington warned:

Be courteous to all, but intimate with few,
and let those few be well tried
before you give them your confidence.
True friendship is a plant of slow growth.

When we choose a friend, we determine the direction of our personality. We hand over to that person an influential power which Sean Connolly describes in his poem *Here's My Life.*

I became a friend and my spirit whispered:
Here's my life, come and make it beautiful
Here's my life, you have the power to change me
Here's my life, you have the chance to hurt me
Here's my life, make it better than I would.

If we cry in self-pity, "No one cares about me," perhaps it is our own fault. We cannot buy the belonging of love. It is something we receive after sharing and spending ourselves. We must be persons who love before we can expect to be loved.

A person who is not loved will have a stunted identity. He'll never be content because being loved is as basic a desire as being alive. Only love can satisfy our thirst for life and refresh our warm feeling of living in hope.

The emptiness and rejection of not being loved is a terrible experience. Yet we ourselves are to blame. Loneliness and unhappiness are born in the recesses of our own selfishness.

Chapter 4

IDENTITY

Every idea is a cause that has an effect. What we think usually makes us what we are. If we are ashamed of what we are becoming, then we should evaluate our ideas.

We cannot determine our destiny, but we do have a choice of an ideology that will influence the direction of our life. We need not be a prisoner of hopeless boredom. The key to freedom and growth is an idea.

In November of 1970 the police found a young girl who had lived in virtual isolation for 13 years. Still clad in diapers, she had the mind of an infant and could not talk. She had been deprived of receiving ideas which would have set off the dynamic evolution of human personality.

We are all born with the raw material of existence. Human contact and an evolution of ideas gradually nurture human life. Our life then expands as our ideas expand.

Erik Erikson has said, "We cannot have an identity without an ideology." The confusion of who we are — our identity — often keeps us ill-at-ease. We search for the meaning and clarification of the "I" in our life. We ask the questions: What values am I seeking? What really counts for me? How am I coming across to other people?

Our philosophy of life sets the tone for our values and goals. Our life then unifies around this fundamental choice with a consistency that keeps order and meaning in our life. Otherwise we'll become confused with thousands of unrelated ideas.

If we are dissatisfied with our identity, then we must reevaluate our ideas. We are what we think. Many people will never be at peace because they have not rearranged and simplified their ideas. They take tranquilizers instead of changing their mentality.

Agere sequitur esse is a Latin phrase which is translated to mean: How you *act* follows what you *are.*

If we are ashamed of our actions, then we should reevaluate our ideas and probe our feelings. Our identity is a natural product of our ideology. We are our ideas so we should be comfortable with them.

> Who, then, is the loneliest one? It is
> the person who is not at home with his
> own thoughts, the one who is alien to
> his own feelings, the one who is a
> stranger to himself — he is the loneliest
> person of all. — Arthur Jersild

Revolutions are provoked by a cultural lag between new ideas and old ideas. It is hoped that the new will be more refreshing than the old. Ideas should evolve. If they do not, it is most probable that they will clash with current culture, causing revolution instead of evolution.

Alvin Toffler in *Future Shock* describes the dizzy disorientation that arises from the superimposition of a new culture on an old one. Ideas should grow gradually. If we stop thinking, change will be a shattering experience.

Crisis and confrontation would be useless words if we only called upon continuity. Marriage problems, the generation gap, and the identity crisis would not be a revolution if we *continued* to evolve and refresh our thinking.

Usually confused action is born from confused ideas. Without adequate thought and preparation, unharnessed activity accomplishes very little.

Our activity then should be guided from a center of reflection deep in the silence of our mind.

We must prepare ourselves by study and know far more than we impart if we expect to convey accurate and responsible ideas.

What we do not have, we cannot give; to act without knowledge only causes confusion.

Quiet reflection dissolves vague uncertainty. Our ideology should be like an iceberg — more hidden below than shown above.

Chapter 5

IDEAS

God gave us two ears and one mouth with the intention, probably, that we listen twice as much as we speak. Ideas happen when we quietly and humbly listen.

G. K. Chesterton says: "Thinking means connecting things." This assimilation requires a certain amount of silence. Ideas breathe in solitude. They expand and envision new horizons. Silence opens up a life that activity has little time or energy to discover.

It takes a lot of energy to think. So we cannot be dissipating it with wasted activity or words. Thinking is an intense experience.

Sit down and take it easy. Feel your thoughts running through your mind. Concentrate on where your ideas come from, what you are doing to them, and how they come out in your expression.

Do not release a dissipated idea. Put your ideas together and make them count.

G. K. Chesterton has stated with comical candor that merely having an open mind is nothing; the object of opening the mind, as of opening the mouth, is to shut it on something solid.

Too often we have allowed ourselves to be satisfied with mediocre ideas and experiences. We open our mind but lack the enthusiastic desire to search after great ideas.

If we are to break the trivia habit, we must touch the great ideas of literature and science. We must start reading — even if it is just the newspaper. The U.N. Statistical Yearbook states that only 305 out of 1,000 people read the newspaper.

Someone once said: "Great men talk about ideas, average men talk about events, and small men talk about people." Without great ideas, we can easily become very small people.

Ideas are not only *its*. The frustration of such a limited definition made Martin Buber cry: "Oh, accumulation of information! It's always it!"

It is easy to build "our ivory tower" of information safe from the availability of people. We protect ourselves from the sensitivity of human feeling with a wall of facts. We fail to appreciate that knowledge is always relational.

The truly educated person has allowed his ideas to become experiences. His pursuit and absorption of truth has refashioned information into people.

It is the opinion of Martin Buber that all real life is meeting people. Everyone we meet is an idea and experience that we should assimilate and absorb. Everyone we meet is another book in our library.

In his book *The Greening of America* Charles Reich points out the significance of generation "consciousness." What one generation assumes is not what the other is conscious of. We are experiencing more of an assumption gap than a generation gap. If we are to bridge this emptiness, we must have an honest and genuine desire to know each other's ideas.

James Burtchaell has written that schism is a breakdown in patience before it is a conflict in creed.

Everyone is in a hurry to make conclusions. If we could only slow down and be patient enough to listen, there could be great possibilities for a unity in diversity.

Usually impatience feeds imprudence, and there is an exchange of distasteful remarks and curt replies. Then the gap becomes larger, and there is little desire to bridge it.

Ideas should be tempered with prudence. A prudent person is quick to think, quick to listen, but slow to speak. He realizes that hasty, rash judgments made by an uninformed mind will only strain emotions and hurt good people. Ideas are too powerful to be rashly spoken.

An electric wire is a very quiet and unassuming dynamism. Touch it and its electrifying current fills our body. An idea has that same power.

Electricity brings us warmth, refreshment, and life, but it can also kill. An idea likewise can destroy us as it did Hitler and Charles Manson. Yet it is also the source of a fruitful and exciting life.

An ideology is powerful, so we must temper it with the Christian message of love. We should ask the question: Are our ideas creating or destroying?

Chapter 6

INVOLVEMENT

Barbra Streisand sings about people who need people being the happiest people in the world. We can *exist* without people, but we cannot *live* without them. But people mean involvement. We must take the risk of being hurt if we are to stay alive. So many of us are dead long before we die.

Once we make the initial decision to deepen our involvement, however, we cannot be afraid to give of ourselves. We truly experience our vitality, our aliveness, our power when we give. Our good intentions cannot remain in the deep recesses of our mind. Along with desire and a sense of risk, participation is the best way to give and get out of ourselves to enjoy life.

"Now" is the time to go out of our way for those who need us. "Yes" is the only protection we have from indifference. Apathy can always find an excuse. It always has a plan to evade involvement. It is false to assume that we'll be happy if we only mind our own business.

The Book of Proverbs stirs our conscience when it says:

Do not refuse a kindness to anyone who asks it if it is in your power to perform it. Do not say, "Go away, come another time! I will give it to you tomorrow," if you can do it *Now*.

We cannot afford to become an "if only" person constantly promising — "if only the conditions were right." If we can say, "Yes," then say it "now" and get involved.

"To be with it" and "right on" are contemporary idioms associated with involvement. They are real words that speak action. They give the feeling that we are in the middle of something important.

Yet involvement must be tempered with solitude if we are to succeed. Adrian van Kaam warns us:

No involvement is possible without detachment, and no detachment is meaningful without a deepening of involvement.

We must occasionally leave the world of involvement to reevaluate the reasons for being involved. Detachment purifies our motives and refreshes our integrity.

When our ideology becomes a selfish pursuit of "pennies, power, and prestige," then it will ultimately destroy us. Detachment is the only guardian of our sanity. It keeps our ideas in proper perspective and keeps us "right on."

35

Frist things must come first. This is the law of priorities which is necessary for a healthy involvement. With only so much time and energy, we must make a decision of what is most important in our life and concentrate on our choice. With a little humility, we can make realistic expectations and not lose perspective.

Our life has many modes. We cannot live them all because we do not have time. So we make a choice — a particular vocation, wife, friends, hobbies — of available modes. As we emphasize one mode of living, others will fade out and become less important.

We are friends, acquaintances, or strangers who are involved in many lives in a cursory manner. If we are truly glad that others are alive and happy, then we'll convey this joy in the intensity of a few passing moments.

We cannot give the intensity of our love to everyone, but we can give the intensity of the present moment. When we are talking to someone, we should act as though this individual is the only person in the world. Anything less than our total awareness and sensitivity will be an injustice to his presence.

Existentialism forms a consciousness that we create ourselves. Unfortunately, it isolates us within our skin. We become preoccupied with our own growth. We pursue our freedom and our authenticity. We are invited to "do our own thing," "do what comes naturally," and "do what we feel is best for ourselves."

Yet there are times when a healthy relationship does not permit us "to do our own thing." It is absolutely impossible to live in constant harmony with others if we do not think of the common good and adjust our personal feelings accordingly.

Involvement cannot survive without compromise. Adjustment, in the form of compromise — especially when it is sacrificial — is not a sign of weakness. What might be good for me, might be harmful to someone else. We cannot talk about our rights if justice is being deprived. We cannot talk about our personal freedom and fulfillment if our quest is only a conquest and our aim is the destruction of another's rights.

Chapter 7

EXPERIENCE

Most of our ideas are usually about experiences — what has happened to us or what has happened to others. Our ideas broaden our vision, but only experiences expand our ideas.

Life is never a waste of time if we are experiencing new, healthy ideas of ourselves. Many times these experiences are gained only in disappointment. We might go to bed one evening with the feeling of accomplishing very little. If we take the time to reflect, however, we'll learn something new from every experience that has happened to us.

"I feel; therefore, I am." A feeling person allows life to penetrate deep into his personality. Reality percolates through every fiber and muscle. He experiences. He savors reality and fully digests real life.

Feeling real life consequently makes us real. We take off the masks and respond with tears, tenderness, touch, or any other emotion that the experience calls forth. Our strength is in our realness.

We can only accomplish one thing at a time. If we are truly convinced of this reality, we'll relax and concentrate with full awareness and responsiveness. After a while, the enjoyment of the present moment will become a habit. So forget the failure of yesterday and the anxiety of tomorrow. Life is the *now. Live intensely* and *venture* into *each* day.

We must *STOP — LOOK* and *LISTEN.* Be alert! What's happening to me right now? Am I feeling the total experience of this moment?

To amass great ideas and have healthy emotions is a far more enriching experience than amassing money.

Someone once said: "Money is like manure. When it is in a pile it stinks, but when it is spread around it helps life grow." Life is more than a savings account to be fought over after our death.

Now is the time to cash our money into experiences. We cannot afford to bankrupt our mind and emotions.

Life is like an onion: You peel it off one layer at a time and sometimes you weep. — Carl Sandburg

If we intend to experience life to its fullest, then we can expect suffering. Our love might be rejected, promises broken, dreams shattered, and health impaired.

But when we write our memoirs, the sweet taste of a full life with its few bitter tears will spell out our experience of satisfaction.

Suffering is not our worst experience. A meaningless life without a sense of satisfaction is the most unbearable.

Use these eight phrases generously, and the experience of love will be magnificent:

I LOVE YOU

I MISS YOU

I AM SORRY

THANK YOU

I AM WRONG

WE FORGET

I FORGIVE

TOGETHER

If we cut our leg, we do not put a bandage over the dirty wound. Hiding it does not heal it. It should be cleaned, even though this may mean further pain. Only then will the infection be stopped in its progress of destroying the whole limb.

Time will heal the many wounds of human experience. But first they should be cleansed with honesty and humility, even though this may mean further pain. Otherwise the infection will linger for a lifetime.

Only two people with the power of reconciliation can venture safely into the experience of mutual, maximum love.

When we love others, we put into their hands the power of hurting us. It is human to hurt, and realistic people are prepared for the friction of interaction. The risk of love is in the power of forgiveness and reconciliation.

"Love is having to say you are sorry." Intimacy will always have its disagreements, but do we have the capacity to be the first to seek out and heal hurt feelings?

This is the true test of reconciliation — to begin again when there appears to be an ending.

What does a person feel in his first experience of eternity? What does he see? What has God prepared for him? If we could revive his human life, would he opt to come back? Is eternity too wonderful to ever return to time? We all wish to know, but we do not want to die to find out.

Death is not *something that happens* to us but a *person who is met*. We will not be afraid of this beautiful experience that awaits us if we are not afraid of God.

The little child in the warmth and comfort of his mother's body is afraid to be born. He has no idea what this other life will be like. Perhaps it is that same fear that we anticipate in death. Unless that child is born, however, he will never feel the love of his parents, see the colors of nature, and enjoy the beauty of sunlight.

Even though we experience many difficulties in this earthly life, we enjoy the comfort of security in the womb of mother earth. We know what we have, and we are afraid to risk the unknown. We feel the same fear as that nine-month-old child in his mother's womb. Unless we are born again in death, however, we'll never experience our greatest happiness.

Chapter 8

ENERGY

If we feel worn out and tired, we are probably wasting our energy. There are three major dissipations: association with negative people, thinking negative thoughts, and engaging in negative conversation.

The negative dissipates our vitality and leaves us bored and angry. Jonathan Livingston Seagull discovered that it was specifically these two traits that shortened a gull's life. It will shorten our life, too.

Our past mistakes and future apprehensions are not considerate of our digestion or sleep — both of which we need to conserve our energy.

Worry dissipates our strength and inhibits the enjoyment and intensity of the present moment.

So break the worry habit — take the risk of being a free person and let God do the worrying. Remember he created you, so rely on his goodness.

When an electric circuit is overloaded, it blows a fuse and leaves the whole house in darkness. We have drained the energy.

Our desires increase more rapidly than our power to produce, and we can easily burn ourselves out with overload. We drain our energy.

We have only so much energy; don't lose it all by overload.

The pursuit of "more and multiple" drives us into a dizzy disorientation that cries for cop outs and escapes.

We clutch to ourselves the burden of our many possessions and sink into the murky waters of emptiness.

As we suffocate the simple beauty of living, we learn too late that happiness is knowing how to be detached and conserve energy.

Organization saves our energy and does not waste our valuable time on nonessentials, overlap, or misdirection. The few hours we spend each week in ordering and preparing our activities will give us the sense of priority and proportion we need to stay in control of our life and conserve our energy.

Organization also gives us the gift of patience and tolerance. We are easily frustrated. But frustration without tolerance becomes imprudent aggression which seeks immediate relief. We strike out in anger to relieve the tension and dissipate our energy with bullying, hostility, revenge, and violence.

"Develop a train of thought on which to ride. The nobility of your life as well as your happiness depends upon the direction in which that train of thought is going." — Dr. Lawrence Peter

When we have developed a philosophy of life, it is easy to make decisions. Energy then enforces each decision.

If we know what we want to accomplish and desire it enough, then neither fear, doubt, nor ridicule can stop us.

"It is impossible without humility to enjoy anything — even pride." — Gilbert Keith Chesterton

Humility is the virtue that reminds us who we are and who we are not. It does not pretend and falsify. It heeds the words of the Psalmist: "Only a breath is any human existence. Like vapor are our restless pursuits."

Humility is a strong virtue; it helps us appreciate the words: "I am only human."

The Book of Sirach informs us: "There is no cure for the proud man's malady since an evil growth has taken root in him." Pride is an obsession which slowly sacrifices values, convictions, and promises. It cannot cope with the feeling of insignificance.

Pride craves power and prestige but it pays the price — by wasting the energy that we need to be truly happy.

Sexual energy is far more than the biological experience of "you service me and I'll service you." Its motivation should be more than a hormonal stimulation. Without a harmonious relationship, sexual energy can give transient pleasure but very little meaning.

A *"meaningful* sexuality" is not a *"me —* sexuality." More than an appetite to be gratified, it is a quality which must be accompanied by responsibility, commitment, and sincere concern.

It is an effective drive away from ourselves and toward the good and happiness of the person we love. Sexuality's most important medium is the brain which helps us to understand that sexual energy expresses a relationship, and is not the relationship itself.

Chapter 9

EXCELLENCE

Excellence is the development of personal potential — not conquest over others.

We are not equal in talent, potential, opportunity, health, or simple good luck. So we strive for relative excellence by setting realistic goals.

The goal is the most important element of excellence as Seneca so wisely reflected:

"When a person does not know what harbor
he is making for, no wind is the right wind."

"If there is one statement true of every living person it must be this: He hasn't achieved his full potential. The latent abilities, hidden talents, and undeveloped capacities for excellence are legion." — William Schutz

The first step toward excellence is to abhor mediocrity. If we sit smug and satisfied in the darkness of apathy, our potential will never see daylight.

"How much more there is to living. Instead of our drab slogging forth and back to the fishing boats, there's a reason to life. We can lift ourselves out of ignorance. We can find ourselves as creatures of excellence, intelligence, and skill. We can be free." — Jonathan Livingston Seagull

"For every job that exists in the world there is someone, somewhere who cannot do it. Given sufficient time and enough promotions, he will arrive eventually at that job and there he will remain — habitually bungling it, frustrating his co-workers, and eroding the efficiency of the organization." — The Peter Principle

Excellence is not the promotion to the top, but the achievement of our competence.

"Appreciation is a wonderful thing. It makes what is excellent in others belong to us as well." — Voltaire

Jealousy retards our growth toward excellence, but the appreciation of another's talent always rubs off and inspires our own enthusiasm to develop our potential.

Excellence is also achieved through affirmation. Dr. Conrad Baars has captured its essence with the reflection:

Affirmation presupposes confident expectation and uninterrupted attention to everything that happens in the other, to all he is not able to express, and to all the anticipated good that lies within.

The very opposite of affirmation is denial. We deny another by reminding him of what is not yet good in him, by thoughtless criticism, or the giving of premature advice without really listening.

Someone has said: "We only live 40 years of life. The rest is only commentary."

Someone else has said: "Today is my moment and now is my story."

The difference between the two is "change and challenge." "C" to it that your life is not merely a commentary of the past.

Our tired cells and deficient hormones should not be an obstacle to our pursuit of excellence.

The problem of growing old is basically one of adjustment and rearrangement. Once we have accepted the reality that we are not as strong and agile as we were years ago, then we can make the positive decision to rearrange our life.

Adjustment is the simple art of changing priorities and developing new potentials. It is never too late to dream and seek the goal of excellence.

Perseverance is the backbone of excellence. It is easy to "cop out" and "give up" with an apathetic cry of self-pity. The pursuit of excellence is difficult, and it takes a courageous person to make the journey.

Courage takes the risk of failure, of making a wrong decision, and of suffering the consequences that follow.

But courage relies on God. It says: "With God on my side, I can do most anything."

Jesus eulogized excellence at the Last Supper:

I have given you glory on earth
by finishing the work you gave me to do.
Do you now, Father, give me glory at your side,
a glory I had with you before the world began.

Chapter 10

THE
ULTIMATE
ANSWER

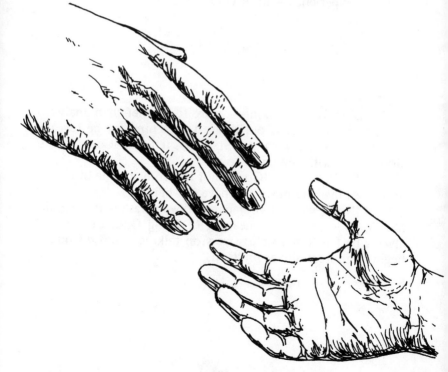

When we break a branch off a vine, it shrivels and the grapes dry up like raisins. It loses its vitality and sustenance.

Jesus Christ testified this would happen when he said: "Remain in union with me and I will remain in union with you. Unless you remain in me you cannot bear fruit, just as a branch cannot bear fruit unless it remains on the vine. I am the vine, you are the branches and so without me you can do nothing."

If you feel like a dried-up raisin, then seek out the ultimate experience — meet God in prayer.

God is a Someone — more to be met than analyzed. He is as close to us as our desire to see him, for he revealed himself as "God is with us." St. James tells us, "Come near to God and he will come near to us."

St. Paul says: "God is not far from anyone of us. For in him we live and move and have our being."

"God, what is your name?" we all ask — hoping, like Moses, to capture the meaning of being God. But we will always be frustrated unless we stop talking about *a* God and begin to address him as *my* God.

Who is God? What is his name? He is what he has done for us. To know God we must discover what he had to say about himself. Open the Scriptures; look around at creation; feel life happening to us. We might not be able to explain life's ultimate meaning; words are so very limited. But eventually we hear ourselves whisper: God.

God once told us his name. He said: "I am who I am." He tells us, in effect, that where everything is, there I am. I am where you are, what you do, what you feel, and what you see.

There is a story told of how God chose to reveal himself to a little girl: "Hi, I'm God," he said. "Do you know who I am?" "Sure," said the girl. "You are the eschatological entity, the Alpha and Omega, the infinite Being that is omnipotent and eternal." And God answered: "Are you sure you have the right person?"

Language searches for adjectives that will describe God. We complicate him with titles and attributes that have filled volumes. God is found in simplicity.

As we enter the mental decompression chamber of our own mind to relax and unwind, our prayer can be as simple as only saying the name of God. We might not wish to talk, but we can listen as our thoughts and dreams reveal his response. We'll begin to feel the vibrations of his presence as we would with anyone who loves us so much.

Our life is torn with such trivia that we need a unity or pattern of growth that will "put it together." Prayer puts the pieces together.

It creates a hub — something that will hold everything together as our ideas and feelings go off in different directions.

We cannot call upon faith unless we have developed its strength and intelligence with prayer.

Faith does not come from will power; it is a gift of God's love in response to our deep relationship with him. We cannot create faith when we need it. We must already have it, and prayer keeps it fresh and vibrant.

Prayer not only gives answers; it also gives direction. It offers a good fusion point for our ideas and feelings to meet and settle differences.

It settles the mind and emotions by quieting the spirit and then proceeds to overcome our anxieties, guilt complexes, and inferiorities by refreshing our faith, assuring forgiveness, and convincing us of our special dignity before God.

God is often part of our pension and Medicare plan because we feel we must have time and leisure to pray. It is certainly preferable that we do enjoy solitude for prayer but this is a luxury. Ordinarily we will find time to talk to God as we talk to people — when we are busy.

The amount of time spent in praying is not essential. Prayer can be instant and spontaneous with the simplicity of just turning our heart and mind to the presence of God.

The Old Testament people did not have a word for prayer. They used the words "sing, rejoice, laugh, and dance." Prayer became the culmination of their total human experience — given to God. Everything they said or did for God was a prayer.

It should be likewise with us. We live to praise God. So the more we appreciate, celebrate, and recreate life around us, the more we praise God.

Other helpful books from Liguori Publications

HOW TO DEVELOP A BETTER SELF-IMAGE
by Russell M. Abata, C.SS.R., S.T.D.
A beautiful "self-help" book that should lead to self-discovery, self-control, and a greater acceptance of self, others, and God. Blends practical psychology with a Christian view of life. $2.95

LOVE YOURSELF
by Edward Richardson, M.M.
Explains that without self-love you cannot love others or be happy and well-adjusted. Shows how you can learn to love yourself without losing the virtues of humility and self-sacrifice. $1.95

FROM VICTIM TO DECISION-MAKER
by Marilyn Norquist Gustin
This book encourages you to trade in a "victim mentality" for the joy and hope and power to choose the quality of your life. The author shares her personal struggle with helplessness and disappointment and shows how even the most painful situations can be made brighter through a change of attitude. She ends each chapter with suggestions for prayer and Scripture readings. $1.95

60 WAYS TO LET YOURSELF GROW
by Martha Mary McGaw, CSJ
A happy, exciting book that shows how to make the most of the precious gift of life. Each page presents a suggestion or project to help the reader open up to life — and includes free space for personal notes. $1.95

BECOMING A NEW PERSON
by Philip St. Romain
Based on the same twelve-step plan used to free people from obsessive-compulsive behavior (drugs, alcohol, etc.), this book offers "healthy" people a way to break free in their spiritual life . . . to become better and happier . . . to become a NEW PERSON. These twelve steps are practical, easy to understand, and offer help by inviting the reader to look inside for strength . . . out to others . . . and beyond to God. $2.95

FINDING GOD IN EVERYDAY LIFE
by Richard A. Boever, C.SS.R.
A simple, practical, contemporary guide to spiritual growth. Readers will discover that they have an abundance of experiences from which to build personal altars for meeting and responding to the Lord. $1.95

See more books and ordering instructions on the next page.